BLACK, BUT NOT MY BROTHER!:

Why I cannot vote for Barack Hussein Obama

authorHOUSE®

AuthorHouse™
1663 Liberty Drive, Suite 200
Bloomington, IN 47403
www.authorhouse.com
Phone: 1-800-839-8640

First published by AuthorHouse 6/11/2009

ISBN: 978-1-4389-2878-4 (sc)

Library of Congress Control Number: 2008909941

Printed in the United States of America
Bloomington, Indiana

This book is printed on acid-free paper.

BY

Donald William Johnson

"*I have a dream that my four little children will one day live in a nation where they will not be judged by the color of their skin but by the content of their character.*"

I Have A Dream
Dr. Martin Luther King, Jr.

August 28, 1963
Washington, D.C

CONTENTS

.

I am indebted to several sources, both print and personal that I've quoted or referenced. Every attention has been given to intentionally acknowledge these sources' implied permission to use. Among them are The Wall Street Journal Online, OneNewsNow.com, Rock Island Argus/ Dispatch, Quad-City Times, Dr. Martin Luther King, Jr., Bishop T. D. Jakes, Pastor Clenard H. Childress, Jr., and Pastor Ken Hutcherson. Any reference not acknowledged is unintentional.

Ef I wuz de President
Of dese United States,
I'd live on 'lasses candy
An' swing on all de gates!

Douglas Dilman,
President of the United States
The Man, by Irving Wallace

It was inevitable that one day America would have to confront the issue of a Black for President, even a Black President. It was 1964 that Irving Wallace published his epoch breaking novel *The Man* which tells the unlikely story of a Black man, Senator Douglas Dilman, an unknown who through multiple tragedies was catapulted by default into the presidency. The President and the Speaker of the House are killed in a freak accident. The Vice-President dies. As president pro-tem of the Senate ("a ceremonial post he was chosen for to appease the party's liberal wing"—that order of succession was before the adoption of the 25th Amendment), Douglas Dilman would succeed to the presidency. An unexpected accident and the law of succession do what the electorate was not willing to do. Dilman was elected senator but none expected him to succeed to the presidency. As President, Dilman "must bear the weight of three burdens: his office, his race, and his private life." As the first Black President, he faces fierce and treacherous opposition. Dilman must "uphold his oath in the face of international crises, domestic dissension, violence, scandal and mean hostility." There was a crisis of confidence, shaped by the stereotype of color. In a time of national crisis, the white political leaders questioned the leadership capabilities and judgment of the Black President. The dramatic conflict is played out before a watching world. The Senate had not met for over one hundred years to do what they intended to do to President Dilman: impeach Him! Just like Andrew Johnson. President Dilman lived.

It was January 25, 1972, eight years after Mr. Wallace published *The Man* that the first Black woman elected to Congress, Shirley Chisolm of New York, announced her candidacy for President of the United States on the Democratic ticket. Congresswoman Chisolm, "Unbought and Unbossed" as her autobiography portrayed her, was the first credible Black candidate for

President of the United States. Later, in 1984 and 1988 the Reverend Jesse Louis Jackson, Sr. of Illinois would run for President. Rev. Al Sharpton also took a run in 2004. But

It was June 5, 2008 that Bishop T. D. Jakes, internationally known pastor of the megachurch The Potter's House in Dallas, Texas wrote about his emotionally moving experience when Senator Barack Hussein Obama gave his victory acceptance speech to become Democratic nominee for President of the United States: "Last night, I like most Americans of all stripes, watched with visible *goose bumps* (italics mine) as history was made. I sat with my 13-year-old son and looked from the screen to his eyes as Sen. Barack Obama became the first African American in history to lead a U. S. major-party ticket when he claimed the nomination for the Democratic Party for president of the United States. I congratulate Sen. Obama on this historic accomplishment..." That same night I, Donald William Johnson, Pastor of Destiny Baptist Church, Rock Island, Illinois remember that my soul responded, too: it shuddered!

Though Bishop Jakes is a Pastor I think highly of, I did not view Mr. Obama's nomination in the same light. Here are my thoughts: five perspectives and my conclusion.

I: Mr. Obama and the challenge of color

Susan Estrich wrote in a viewpoint column that "Race too costly to be a factor in upcoming election," Quad-City Times, A17, June 15, 2008. However, race is a real issue. "One third of all voters say the candidates' race will be a factor in their vote, with 48 per cent of blacks saying it will be an important factor and 20 percent saying it will be the single most important factor," McCain making play at NAACP for votes Obama Should win, by William Douglas, McClatchy Newspapers, 7/13/08). Race affects not only Whites but Blacks as well. For Blacks, race is more a factor than we realize. And certainly more than we're ready to admit. Black America is so intoxicated by the thought that America might elect a Black President that we're willing to sell our collective soul for the presidency. We've been so blinded by our identify with Blackness that we've ignored the often quoted, haunting words of Dr. Martin Luther King, Jr. about his dream of a world "where people will be judged not by the color of their skin but the content of their character." This election will certainly expose the sincerity of the soul of the Black community across the country. We're all looking toward this historic day. I think the following invitation puts it in perspective:

"_____ will be open at 6 p.m. on November 4th—election night. We'll watch the returns come in and hopefully will celebrate the historic election of Barack Obama or be pi_ _ed off if America doesn't *"get it right"* (italics mine). Rock Island, Illinois.

There is excitement in Black America-a pregnant pulsation for the political.

In the Black community today, as I write, if one is Black it is *expected and assumed* that one is voting for Mr. Obama. Mr. Obama is Black. Black Democrats are ecstatic. The Democratic Party is seeking to register Black voters in Southern states like Alabama and Georgia. These newly registered voters are expected to vote as Black people and to vote for Mr. Obama, a Black man. The White House is in view—even with a Black man as the nominee.Black Republican conservatives are so emotionally divided that they're so tempted to cross party lines and vote Democratic that they are even reluctant to criticize Mr. Obama's positions--because he is Black. It is expected that because Mr. Obama has Black skin that Black people will defend him and vote for him, regardless. At the same time, even though some high profile Black Republicans disagree with him philosophically they're tempted to vote color rather than conservative. Noteworthy are former talk-show host Armstrong Williams, Congressman J.C. Watts (R—Oklahoma), and former Secretary of State Colin Powell. Commentator Armstrong Williams confesses their dilemma, "Among Black conservatives, they tell me privately, it would be *very hard to vote against him* (Barack Obama) *in November* (italics mine)" <u>Conservatives consider voting for Obama</u>," The Rock Island Argus, (6/15/08, page A9). Mr. Williams has a second problem. His "82-year-old mother, who also hasn't voted for a Democratic candidate, has already made up her mind...She is so proud of Senator Barack Obama, and she has made it clear to all of us that she's voting for him in November...Because she said, given the history of this country, she never thought she'd ever live to see this," <u>Conservative blacks leaning towards Obama</u>, by Frederic J. Frommer, Associated Press Writer, OneNewsNow.com, 6/15/2008. This intended defection is getting the kind of attention Congressman John Lewis received when he switched allegiance from Senator Hillary Clinton to Senator Barack Obama. Two Black conservatives reacted to the announcement that these prominent Black Republicans were considering voting for Mr. Obama November 4th. Their primary argument is that the election "should be about character, they say, not skin color." Pastor Ken Hutcherson of Antioch Bible Church of suburban Seattle, Washington contends that Black "conservatives who are supporting Democratic presidential candidate Barack Obama must remember what they have been saying about race for decades," <u>Black 'conservatives" blasted for pro-Obama remarks</u>, by Jeff Johnson and Chad Groening, OneNewsNow.com, 6/19/08. Have Blacks not quoted the mellifluous words of Dr. Martin Luther King, Jr. to White people: "I have a dream that my four little children will one day live in a nation where they will not be judged by the color of their skin but by the content of their character."

Pastor Hutcherson continues that "he understands being proud of a black man, but he notes that for years black conservative leaders have screamed that it is not about color…it's about the content and character of one's heart. "…(A) nd some of these same guys seem to be forgetting that's what we're supposed to be doing now," says Hutcherson. (Ibid.) When Armstrong Williams contends that history "thrusts" him to consider Mr. Obama, Pastor Hutcherson responds that "African-Americans need to forget about their 'blackness' and talk about what they can do as citizens of the United States…(T)here will always be a race problem," the pastor maintains. "But conservatives vote on what is right and wrong…Williams is forgetting that principle because he is *excited about Obama's skin color* (Italics mine)"…

(A)nd I think that that is absolutely wrong," he reprimands (Ibid.). Pastor Hutcherson boldly declares that he "will not support any candidate, regardless of party or race, who does not support biblical values." On the other hand, Black politician "former Maryland Lieutenant Governor Michael Steele says he is proud of Obama as a black man, but he will do everything in his power to keep the senator out of the White House," (Ibid.). Jesse Lee Peterson, founder and President of the Brotherhood Organization of a New Destiny in Los Angeles concurs with Hutcherson and Steel but in a more pointed statement. Peterson "doesn't care about being part of an historic moment...There's no way that I can vote for Barack Obama simply *because of a historic moment and he is a black man* (Italics mind). That doesn't make sense to me," he says. "We should judge people based on character and not color or historic moment." (Ibid.) Mr. Peterson makes a final indicting comment "There are a lot of black Republicans who are not real Republicans," he says bluntly. They're in the party because they believe that blacks should be in both parties and they want to influence (the GOP) in a way that Democrats would influence it—not necessarily because they're Republicans," <u>Black 'conservatives' blasted for pro-Obama remarks</u>, OneNewsNow. com, by Jeff Johnson and Chad Groening, 6/19/08.

In the face of Mr. Obama's color not only Black conservative Republicans but many Black religious leaders ignore his positions to the future detriment not only to Black people but to America. Black pastors in Chicago "support" Senator Obama, (Quad City Times,

5/3/08, page A5). Other religious leaders and groups lend him support as well.The political action committee Matthew 25 produced and aired a television ad "that is reportedly the first of its kind recorded by active clergy members for a Democratic presidential candidate...(the) ad called 'Families,' featuring emergent church leader Brian McLaren and Methodist mega-church pastor Kirbyjohn Caldwell," ("Obama's 'clergy ad' avoids biblical issues", Jim Brown, Onenewsnow.com, 8/20/08). The ads show Mr. Obama family friendly even though he holds positions that are against the family. However, Carrie Gordon Earll of Focus on the Family offers an opposing view of the Matthew 25 production. The "ad is an extension of the Democratic party's effort since 2006 to court religious conservative voters...The question I would think that religious leaders would be asking is, what is this man's view on issues? What's his Christian worldview on issues?" (Ibid) Earll argues that if Bible-believing Christians—those in the pews and those in the pulpits—really knew Obama's stance on abortion, for example, they would understand why there is no way they could support his candidacy. She concludes, "I don't think that most pastors in this country--(those) who believe the Bible is the Word of

God and interpret that through what we know is traditional Christian worldview—are going to be able to just close their eyes to the radical pro-abortion position of Senator Obama...This is a man who has pledged to sign a Freedom of Choice Act that would overturn every pro-life law—state, local, national—in the nation," (Ibid). Nevertheless, other religious leadership includes the very prominent Randy and Paula White of the Without Walls Church in Tampa, Florida who are "supporting Barack Obama". (Onenewsnow.com, 8/24/08).

A telling example of this looking but not seeing is that of Minister Louis Farrakhan. Minister Farrakhan of the Nation of Islam was recently recognized as "Man of the Year" at Trinity United Church of Christ in Chicago, formerly pastored by. Dr. Jeremiah Wright, Mr. Obama's former church and former pastor. (To my knowledge, we don't know whether the Obama family does public worship anywhere, anymore). Minister Farrakhan spoke at the Nation of Islam annual convention that Senator Obama is the *"hope of the entire world"* (italics mine), Associated Press. According to the AP report, "Farrakhan spent most of a nearly two-hour speech praising Obama." Rev. Clinard

Childress (Pastor of New Calvary Baptist
Church, Montclair, New Jersey and founder of
the website <u>BlackGenocide.org</u>) "spoke that Mr.
Farrakhan's strong backing of Mr. Obama shows
'deception upon deception...Has Islam chosen
to ignore Obama's advocacy of men having sex
with men, and women with women?", questions
Childress. "I would like to know, has Islam also
decided to join with Barack Obama and the
abortion industry and the wholesale killing of
babies in the womb? Are we asked now to ignore
our faith and our conscience? This is sad." Is
not what Minister Farrakhan doing what many
other Americans, especially Black Americans,
are doing--setting aside our values in favor of
the prospect of political victory: the first Black
President—(no slight intended against former
President Bill Clinton, America's first "Black
President"). Pastor Childress continues, "It's
obvious that Louis Farrakhan is riding the
present popularity of Barack Obama, but yet
once again at the expense of his own values...
values that I understood Islam held...But yet
such is most of America, and those who are
advocating Barack Obama's...candidacy are
also forgetting their values." For the Black
community which is under genocidal attack by
Planned Parenthood, one cannot but agree with

Childress that "Obama's support for abortion alone makes the Illinois Senator unfit to be President."

In the face of Mr. Obama's color, many Blacks echo the dramatic testimony of an unknown poet(ess):

"Today, I cried......I voted for a black man and I cried.

I cried for my father and my grandfather

And all the grandfathers before him.

I cried for my uncles, my four brothers, my seventeen nephews, my

two sons, my six grandsons and one great-grand son.

I cried for the black I have loved and those that loved me.

I cried for the millions of little black boys (not forgetting the girls)

Over the centuries that did not, in their wildest dreams imagine...that

They

Could run for Office. I cried for their despair..I cried for all the men

And
Boys incarcerated that lost hope in
themselves and took the low road.
> *I cried, I cried and I cried..*

I know that this was "just the primary."
But whatever the end
> *Result may be, today I voted in the*
United States of America
> *For a black man, and I..cried.*
If I should die before the presidential
election it will be OK,
> *Because today I voted. I voted for a black*
man and I cried."

After reading this poem, I cried, too. But my crying was for Mr. Obama, because he is a Black man. As a Black man, a Black husband, a Black father, a Black Christian and a Black pastor I expected more and different. I cannot vote for a "Black" man or other who supports abortion—which has taken the lives since 1973 of over 45,000,000 babies in America and , including 15,000,000 Black babies—one fourth of the Black community exterminated—and the consequent babies not born because their parents had been aborted. I cried for a father who hates children—who supports partial birth abortion and four times voted against the Born Alive Infants Protection Act which would have allowed medical care for a baby who survived an abortion. As a Black father I cried for him because I agonize for this young man whose father deserted him--and left him as if he had been aborted. I cried for this particular Black man who supports not only domestic partnership but so-called "homosexual-marriage" when the killer in the Black community second only to abortion is AIDS—the most affected being Black women and Black babies. I cried because he asked me to vote for him to be my President. I cried because he expects me to vote for him because I am Black-- and he is "Black."

The question has been asked, "Is he Black?" The question has been asked, "Is he Black enough?" If Black is his color, he is. But, if Black is more than that, he is NOT! Black skin color alone cannot be trusted to authenticate Blackness. Blackness is more than the color of the skin.

Black skin color cannot be trusted as an unimpeachable shibboleth. Judges 12:1-7, especially 5b-6 is the basis for our thought (see II Corinthians 11:14). The Gileadites had defeated the Ephramites at war. When the defeated Ephramites wanted to pass through the Gileadites at the Jordan fords, pretending to be Gileadites, they would be asked to say "shibboleth." Because the Ephramites could not pronounce the sibilant in Shibboleth they would say Sibboleth, exposing them to be Ephramites rather than Gileadites. You can't always trust what you see to be what it looks like to you.

Jesus asked the question, "Who is my mother, my brothers, or my sisters?", Matthew 12:46-50. This is a critical question for Black people today. The Gileadites realized that the Ephramites were not brothers but enemies. The Gileadites used language to expose their enemies. Jesus gave a different definition to family. Jesus would even go so far as to say "Those who are not against me are for me," Luke 9:50.

The image of blackness, complexion, and outward appearance is Black by words but not by will. This is one who is Black by default not by desire—the Black who is inescapably Black imprisoned against his will in this prison of pigmentation: he's born Black. There are many

Blacks who pass for White, because they prefer not to be Black.

Traditionally we, both the larger white world and the closer Black world, have used the visible for verification of identity when it is only evidence of image. The real Black may not be the looks like Black. The real Black may not even live in the ghetto, where all Blacks are supposed to live. The person who lives in "the hood" may not be your brother but your enemy. He shares your color but not your soul, your inner identity. It seems appropriate to borrow a line from the Prophet Samuel when he went to Jesse the Bethlemite's house to seek and set aside the successor to King Saul. Like us, in a world of hegemony Samuel expected Jesse's oldest boy Eliab to ignite the anointing oil for his anointing as the coming new king. Samuel spoke quietly, silently to himself, "Surely the LORD'S anointed is before Him." But the listening LORD made the powerful statement, "Do not look on his appearance or on the height of his stature, because I have rejected him; for the LORD sees not as man sees; man looks on the outward appearance but the LORD looks on the heart," I Samuel 16:6-7. God's anointed was the last and the least among the brothers, the reject, the youngest, David.

We must look not at Mr. Obama's "outward appearance", his color, but "on the heart", his beliefs. Mr. Obama looks good, until he speaks. Mr. Obama sounds good, until we listen to what he says.

You may live in my neighborhood but not be for me. You may live next door to me but not be my neighbor. You may share the same mother with me on our birth certificates but that not be enough to make us love one another. You may share the same father with me to have a common last name but still not be enough to hold us together as family. You may live on my street but long to live on another street in another neighborhood.

The identity of blackness, character, and inwardness where one is Black by walk and not just by words. Being Black is more than eating collard greens and high fiving. Being Black is more than being the child to a Black man and a White woman. Being Black is about being and doing what's best for the Black community, as a part of the larger community. As Rev. Henry Biggs told entrepreneur Mr. Joe

Hamilton when Mr. Hamilton had gotten the deed to St. Matthew's Baptist Church with the plans to demolish the church to replace it with a modern, technologically upscale church and housing: "You're not for the things that we're for", The Preacher's Wife.

This book is designed to identify some issues for us to think about before we vote. All attention is now on the most well known Black in America, and possibly the world: Barack Hussein Obama, the grandson of Madelyn Dunham, the son of Stanley Ann Dunham Obama, and the husband of Michelle Obama. He is the son of a Black African father from Kenya, Africa—who abandoned him as many Black fathers have done in America. He is the son of a white woman who divorced his father; a woman who was disenchanted with organized religion. Barack Hussein Obama is the son of a Black man, Barack Hussein Obama, Sr. but he is also the son of a White woman—who raised him "in her image and likeness." Barack was raised by his mother but wrote his memoir about his father—Dreams From My Father. "Obama is his mother's son," wrote Amanda Ripley, <u>A mother's</u> Story, Time, page 36, April 21, 2008. It is understandable that he talks more like a

White woman than a Black man. Ralph Nader says he "talks white."

II. Mr. Obama and faith

We're so fixated by Mr. Obama's color that we've not listened clearly and critically of his understanding of what it means to be a Christian. He does have a faith position. Senator Obama told an audience in Greensboro, North Carolina that he was a Christian. He told them that "although he believes Christ died for his sins, those who reject that teaching can also be children of God", Obama contends belief in Jesus Christ not necessary for salvation, OneNewsNow.com, 3/27/08. Mr. Obama "told the audience that he believes he '*can* (italics mine) have everlasting life' because Jesus Christ died for his sins. But he then told a questioner that he believes Jews and Muslims who live *moral lives* (italics mine)are just as much 'children of God' as he is. (He) added that his late mother didn't share his faith but was a kind and generous person, so he's '*sure that she's in heaven* (italics mine)" (Ibid).

In a 2004 interview with Chicago Sun Times religion editor Cathleen Falsani for her book The God Factor: Inside the Spiritual Lives of Public People Mr. Obama told her, "I'm rooted in the Christian *tradition* (italics mine). I believe there are *many paths to the same place* (italics mine), and that a belief that there is a *higher power* (italics mine), a belief that we are connected as a people," Obama numbered among the false prophets, Jody Brown, OneNewsNow.com, 6/18/08. Ms. Falsani quotes John 14:6 to Mr. Obama where "Jesus says of Himself, 'I am the way and the truth and the life. No one comes to the Father except through me.' That sounds exclusive, but Obama says *it depends on how this verse is heard* (italics mine). According to Falsani, Obama thinks that 'all people of faith—Christians, Jews, Muslims, animists, everyone—know the same God.' (Her words)," Obama is no Joshua, by Cal Thomas, Tribune Media Services, CalThomas.com, June 16, 2008. Mr. Thomas asks a very perceptive question. "Evangelicals and serious Catholics might ask if this is so, why did Jesus waste His time coming to Earth, suffering pain, rejection and crucifixion? If there are many ways to God, He might have sent down a spiritual version of table manners and avoided the rest,"(Ibid). Mr.

Obama tells Ms. Falsani, "The difficult thing about religion, including Christianity, is that at some level there is a call to evangelize and proselytize. There's the belief, certainly is some quarters, that if people haven't embraced Jesus Christ as their personal savior, they're going to hell...I can't imagine that my God would allow some little Hindu kid in India who never interacts with the Christian faith to somehow burn for all eternity. That's just not part of my makeup." Falsani adds, "Obama doesn't believe he, or anyone else, will go to hell. But he's not sure he'll be going to heaven, either." (Ibid)

"I don't presume to have knowledge of what happens after I die. When I tuck in my daughters at night and I feel like I've been a good father to them, and I see that I am transferring values that I got from my mother and that they're kind people and that they're curious people, that's a little piece of heaven," (Ibid). When asked, "Who's Jesus to you?" He states, "Jesus is an historical figure for me, and he's also a bridge between God and man, in the Christian faith, and one that I think is powerful precisely because he serves as that means of us reaching *something higher* (italics mine)." NOTICE THAT HE DOES NOT SAY JESUS

IS MY SAVIOR OR JESUS IS LORD! YET HE GOES ON: "And he's also a wonderful teacher. I think it's important for all of us, of whatever faith, to have teachers in the flesh and also teachers in history," <u>Is Barack Obama Really A Christian,</u> http://sub-h.com/obamachristian. htm, excerpt from Falsani interview. When asked about heaven, "He goes on to explain, 'What I believe in is that if I live my life as well as I can, that I will be rewarded," (Ibid). Mr. Thomas refers to Mr. Obama's "works salvation" when he concludes "Obama can call himself anything he likes, but there is a clear requirement for one to qualify as a Christian and Obama doesn't meet that requirement. One cannot deny central tenets of the Christian faith, including the deity and uniqueness of Christ as the sole mediator between God and Man and be a Christian. Such people do have a label applied to them in Scripture. They are called 'false prophets,," (Ibid).

According to an Associated Press statement Bishop Jakes and several ministers met behind closed doors in Chicago June 10th where "Obama took questions, listened to participants and discussed his 'personal journey of faith'." <u>Jakes part of closed-door meeting with Obama</u>,

Associated Press, OneNewsNow.com, 6/11/08).
Up to this point, I'm not aware that the meeting
influenced any position revisions. Mr. Obama's
thinking sounds like universalism, which means
all will be saved, regardless of belief. However
New Testament teaching is that salvation is a
universal offering, which means that there is
an invitation for all to believe and confess faith
in God through Jesus Christ. So, is Mr. Obama
really a Christian?

III.Mr. Obama and abortion

We've ignored Senator Obama's positions on abortion. 50 million babies are killed worldwide every year. In America, abortion kills 3200 Americans per day, that's 1,200,000 per year. In America, 90 % of Downs Syndrome babies are aborted, according to Dr. James Dobson, Focus on the Family. Abortions for rape and incest account for less than 3% of abortions. There are other reasons for all other abortions. Every day in America 1452 Black babies are routinely murdered by abortion. In America, a baby is aborted every 22 seconds. In America, one Black baby is aborted every minute, every day. In America, one of every two Black babies is aborted (The Centers for Disease Control). Every hour of every day in America Black babies die by abortion. There is a disproportionate killing of Black babies in their mother's womb (We'll refer later to Margaret Sanger and Planned Parenthood's agenda of genocide to "exterminate" Blacks through sterilization and abortion). Since 1973 and the Supreme Court's judicial fiat legislation of and legalization of abortion by demand in its Roe v Wade ruling, more than 45,000,000 babies have died through on demand abortion. Of the 45,000,000 aborted babies 15,000,000 Black babies have died in America's holocaust-- 25% of Black America has been exterminated by abortion. From 1882-1968 the Ku Klux Klan lynched over 3,000 Black men. If 1452 Black babies are aborted daily, every three days in America over 4,000 Black babies are, in the words of Dr. Johnny M. Hunter of Life Education and Research Network, Inc., "womb-lynched" by abortion, more than deaths by the Ku Klux Klan. Black women constitute 13% of the female population in the United States, but they underwent nearly 38% of the abortions. According to the Alan Guttamacher Institute, Black women are more than 3 times as likely as white women to have an abortion. It deserves repeating that 80% of Planned Parenthood Clinics are in the minority neighborhoods. Our nation is in trouble; the Black community is in real trouble. Abortion threatens our very existence, even as it once threatened the future of Israel.

For the religious, genocide by abortion was not the original thinking of the eugenicist Margaret Sanger, founder of Planned Parenthood, but is predated by Pharoah Seti I of Egypt. His royal directive for Israelite population control, especially who Claude Brown calls "The Manchild," (Manchild In the Promised Land, by Claude Brown) resembles America's partial birth abortion (Exodus 1:15-22). Whatever the manner, there was neither a Partial Birth Ban nor was there a Born Alive Infant Protection Act. Back to our president predicament.

As a presidential candidate, Senator Obama chose a pro-abortion Roman Catholic as his Vice-Presidential running mate: Senator Joseph Biden of Delaware. Since 1973's Supreme Court ruling in Roe vs Wade permitting abortion on demand, 15,000,000 Black babies have been killed—that's 25 % of the Black race has been destroyed by abortion. Senator Obama opposed both the Illinois and United States Born Alive Infant Protection Act, which protects the life of a baby who survives an abortion. He is a supporter of infanticide. Mr. Obama has said that "the *first (*italics mine) thing that I'd do as president is sign The Freedom of Choice Act"(Planned Parenthood Action Fund, July 17, 2007)—

'which would overturn hundreds of federal and state laws limiting abortion , including the federal ban on partial birth abortion and bans on public funding of abortion.' Certainly, this would include opposition, too, to parental notification and parental consent before a minor girl could get an abortion. Because he believes that abortion is "reproductive justice...one of the most fundamental rights we have," <u>The Audacity of Death,</u> by Daniel Elliott, The Wall Street Journal Online, 6/5/08).

Planned Parenthood and NARAL (National Abortion Rights Action League) have endorsed Mr.Obama. Planned Parenthood is the leading abortion provider in America. 80% of the Planned Parenthood clinics are in minority neighborhoods. Planned Parenthood was started by the eugenicist Margaret Sanger. Margaret Sanger was a white supremacist, who philosophically identified not only with the radical Austrian anti-Semite Adolph Hitler and the eugenicist Thomas Malthus but also the Ku Klux Klan. She spoke to the Klan. They were all involved in racial politics which sought to enforce population control determined by race. Margaret Sanger felt that Whites were superior to Blacks, Hispanics (Roman Catholics) and

Jews. And that the populations of these groups should be controlled and/or be reduced. That these groups were "dysgenic," that they were like "weeds", which needed to be destroyed. Dr. Clarence Gamble, heir of Proctor and Gamble, wrote a memorandum in November, 1939 entitled: <u>"Suggestions for the Negro Project."</u> In the letter he suggested *black leaders "be placed in positions where it would appear they were in charge,"* <u>Margaret Sanger Would Have Loved Barack</u> Obama, by Rev. Clenard H. Childress, http://blackgenocide.org/obama.html, page 1, March 5, 2008. In this so called Negro project Margaret Sanger sought to use Black preachers to encourage Black women to get sterilized or have abortions. Margaret Sanger sought to use Black preachers to destroy Black women in the same way that David used Joab to eliminate Uriah the Hittite, II Samuel 11:14-25. Her strategy was outlined in a letter back to Dr. Gamble, heir of Proctor and Gamble, "We should hire three or four colored ministers, preferably with social-service backgrounds, and with engaging personalities. The most successful educational approach to the Negro is through a *religious appeal* (italics mine). We don't want the word to get out that we want to exterminate the Negro population and the *minister is the man who can straighten out that idea if it ever occurs to any of their more rebellious members,"* (Sanger, Margaret. Letter to Clarence J. Gamble, M.D. December 10, 1939. Sanger manuscripts, Sophia Smith Collection, Smith College, North Hampton, Massachusetts).

We must understand the parallels between abortion and slavery. The underlying philosophy is the same: oppression of Black people. In 1977, Rev. Jesse Jackson, Sr. wrote a 1000 word essay to the National Right to Life News:

"There are those who argue that the right to privacy is of higher order than the right to life. I do not share that view. I belief that life is not private, but rather it is public and universal. If one accepts the position that life is private, and therefore you have the right to do with it as you please, one must also accept the conclusion of that logic. That was the premise of slavery. You could not protest the existence or treatment of slaves on the plantation because that was private and therefore outside of your right to concerned. "Another area that concerns me greatly, namely because I know how it has been used with regard to race, is the psycholinguistics involved in this whole issue of abortion. If something can be dehumanized through the rhetoric used to describe it, then the major battle has been won…Those advocates of taking life prior to birth do not call it killing or murder; they call it abortion. They further talk about aborting a baby because that would imply something human. Rather they talk about aborting the fetus. Fetus sounds less than human and therefore can be justified. "What happens to the mind of a person, and the moral fabric of a nation, that accepts the aborting of the life of a baby without a pang of conscience? What kind of a person, and what kind of a society will have 20 years hence if life can be taken so casually?"

Black Leadership Owes Don Imus An Apology: African-American Leadership Mum on Planned Parenthood, by Rev. Clenard H. Childress, BlackNews.com, 5/12/08.

ABORTION & SLAVERY

ROE VS. WADE 1973	DRED SCOTT 1857
7-2 Decision	7-2 Decision
Unborn: Non-person	Black slave: Non-person
Property of Owner	Property of Owner
(Mother) Choose to Keep or Kill	(Master) Choose to Buy-Sell-Kill
Pro-Lifers Should Not Impose	Abolitionists Should Not Impose
Morality on Mother	Morality on Slave Owner
Abortion is Legal	Slavery is Legal

(Human Life Alliance © 2008, page 4)

"Personally, I don't believe in slavery", they say. "As a Christian, I believe it's wrong," they say. "However, I must not inflict my morality on others," they say. "Therefore, it's alright for you to be a slave-master if you choose," they say. They say. In like manner, Senator Biden said, "I'm prepared as a matter of faith to accept that life begins at the moment of conception. But that is my judgment," Biden said on NBC's Meet the Press." "For me to impose that judgment on everyone else who is equally and maybe even more devout than I am seems to me inappropriate in a pluralistic society," <u>Obama says he was too flip on abortion question,</u> Associated Press, OneNewsNow.com, 9/8/08. Yet, Mr. Obama says that "Secularists are wrong when they ask believers to leave their religion at the door before entering into the public square. Frederick Douglass, Abraham Lincoln, William Jennings Bryan, Dorothy Day, Martin Luther king—indeed, the majority of great reformers in American history—were not only motivated by faith but repeatedly use religious language to argue for their cause. *To say that men and women should not inject their 'personal morality' into public policy debates is a practical absurdity," (*Italics mine), <u>Obama, Religion and the Public Square</u>, by William McGurn, The Wall Street Journal, 6/11/08.

In effect, then my personal morality ought to determine my public policy.

It must inform our priorities and positions. In some cases, we must consider becoming single issue voters. For instance, if you asked Frederick Douglass if he was a single issue voter he would probably say "Yes, if the issue is slavery." Today, I believe we as Black people must see the genocide of Black people through abortion being our most important concern. It is about Black survival and Black advancement.

Akua Furlow calls Planned Parenthood's genocidal attack upon the Black community "reproductive racism." In 2002, a group of Blacks filed a class action suit in the U. S. District Court in St. Louis against Planned Parenthood Federation of America and Planned Parenthood of St. Louis. The suit alleges medical malpractice, wrongful death, civil rights violations, mass fraud, and genocide by specifically targeting minority women for abortions. Mr. Obama, Black leaders, and civil rights organizations were outraged over the Don Imus situation when Mr. Imus made critical racial comments towards members of the Rutgers Women's Basketball team. But there was only silence when it was reported that Planned Parenthood willingly, knowingly took contributions from people to abort Black babies for racial reasons. A person pretending to be a racist donor requesting their donation be used to abort specifically Black babies taped the conversation with the Planned Parenthood representative, Autum Kersey, Vice President of

Development at Planned Parenthood of Idaho. The donor's question was whether a donation could be given for the abortion of a "black baby." Listen to the dialogue:

Idaho donor: Hello, Autum, I'm interested in making a donation today.

Kersey: Fantastic!

Idaho donor: What about abortions for the underprivileged minority Groups?

Kersey: Oh, absolutely.We have, um, in fact, uh wonderful, fantastic news.We just received a very generous donation to our woman in need fund.

Idaho donor: Wonderful.I want to specify that abortion to help a minority group—would that be possible?

Kersey: Absolutely.

Idaho donor: OK, so the abortion.I can give money specifically for a black baby, that would be the purpose?

Kersey: Absolutely.If you wanted to designate your gift be used to help (an) African-American woman in need, then we would certainly make sure that the gift was earmarked specifically for that purpose.

Idaho donor: Great, because I really faced trouble with affirmative action, and I don't want my kids to be disadvantaged, you know, against black kids.I just had a baby.I want to put it in his name, you know.

Kersey: Mmhmm, absolutely.

Idaho donor: So that's definitely possible.

Kersey: Oh, always, always

Idaho donor: So I just wanna—can I put this in the name of my son?

Kersey: Absolutely.

Idaho donor: Yeah, he's trying to get into college, and he's going to be applying, you know, he's justwe're just really big he's really faced troubles with affirmative action.

Kersey: Mmhmm

Idaho donor: And we don't, you know, we just think, you know, the less black kids out there the better.

Kersey: (Laughs) Understandable, understsandable...Um David, let me, if I may, just get some sort of specific general information so we can set this up the right way. You said you wanted to put it in your son's name, and you would like this designated specifically to assist (an) African American woman who's looking to terminate a pregnancy.

Idaho donor: Exactly, and yeah.I wanna protect my son, so he can get into college.

Kersey:Alright.Excuse my hesitation, um, um, this is the first time I've had a donor call and make this kind of request, so I'm excited, and I wanna make sure I don't leave anything out.

(listen to the whole transcript, released by The Advocate. By Sandra Foster-
  sforester@idahostatesman.com, 2/28/08).

Though this dialogue is "far more insidious and notorious than Don Imus could ever be, Black Leadership has done nothing to end these blatant acts of bigotry and racism perpetrated against the African-American community by Planned Parenthood. You would think an African-American candidate for the presidency of the United States, who suggested the firing of a fading cowboy over his racially charged comments, would respond to this alarming evidence of injustice and bigotry. But no!" , Black Leadership Owes Don Imus An Apology: African-American Leadership Mum on Planned Parenthood, by Rev. Clenard H. Childress, Jr., BlackNews.com, May 12, 2008. There was no repudiation of Planned Parenthood's endorsement by Senator Obama. No civil rights leader or civil rights group called for the reprimand and/or firing of Ms. Kersey. More than likely, Ms. Kersey is still taking blood money to exterminate Black babies.

Mr. Obama is double-tongued on life, duplicitous especially as to when life begins. At Apostolic Church of God in Chicago, Mr. Obama told the Father's Day congregation that "we need *fathers* to realize that responsibility doesn't *just end at conception* (italics mine)."

Mr. Obama went on to chastise, to what Rev. Jesse Jackson called "talking down" to the Black community. "That doesn't just make you a father. What makes you a man is not the ability to have a *child.* Any fool can have a child. *It's the courage to raise a child that makes you a father* (italics mine)." (Essence, September 2008, page 156). However, in the forum at Saddleback Church when asked regarding the question of life's beginning, Mr. Obama disingenuously answered that "the question was above my pay grade," (AP, 9/8/08). . Essentially a non answer for the Senate's "most liberal member," and on the issue of abortion even to the left of Senator Hillary Clinton.

Mr. Obama declares that he is a Christian, even though he does not read his Bible as "regularly as I would like. These days I don't have much time for reading or reflection, period," Is Barack Obama Really A Christian, excerpt from Falsani interview). Therefore, I've collected several Biblical references on the beginning of and integrity of human life for Senator Obama to consider: Genesis 1:26-31; Genesis 25:19-26; Exodus 21:22-25. Psalm 139:13-18; Jeremiah 1:5-10; Galatians 1:15-16; and John 3:16. Since 1973, how many Jeremiah's or Apostle Paul's have been aborted? What about a Julian Bond or a Jesse Jackson, Sr.? Speaking of Rev. Jesse Jackson, Sr. he's changed his position on abortion (see above 1977 letter to National Right to Life).

Planned Parenthood and National Abortion Rights Action League give him a one hundred percent 'pro-choice" rating because of his votes against any and all restrictions on late-term abortions and parental involvement in teenagers' abortions," <u>The Audacity of Death,</u> by Daniel Allott, The Wall Street Journal Online, June 5, 2008. NARAL moved its support from Senator Clinton to Senator Obama because he was more pro abortion than Senator Clinton. Abortion activist Frances Kissling is reported to have said Mrs. Clinton was "not radical enough on abortion," <u>The Audacity of Death</u>, by

Daniel Allott, The Wall Street Journal Online, June 2, 2008.

Mr. Obama is for unrestricted abortion: abortion in any form, from surgical/chemical to partial birth; and at any time—even after birth. Senator Obama has an unrelenting commitment to abortion. He's for partial birth abortion, which is the most barbaric medical procedure in medical malpractice. (See Michelle Obama's February 17, 2004 fund raising letter). Let me give you a description of Partial-Birth Abortion, sometimes called Dilation and Extraction. "After undergoing two days of dilation, the abortionist performs an ultrasound to locate the child's legs and feet. The abortionist then uses a large forceps to grasp one of the baby's legs. He pulls firmly, forcing the child into a feet down position (*the baby is turned by the abortionist so that the head is no longer naturally positioned to exit the mother's body first,* italics mine)…Using his hands instead of forceps, the abortionist delivers the baby's body in a manner similar to a breech birth. The baby's head remains inside the birth canal. The abortionist uses surgical scissors to pierce the child's head at the base of the skull. The scissors are forced open to enlarge the skull opening. The abortionist then inserts a suction catheter *into the brain and vacuums out the child's brain tissue with a* (italics not mine) machine 29 times more powerful than a household vacuum," Abortion Methods, Human Life Alliance©2008, page 4. Partial birth abortion is the most gruesome of the some six methods used to kill babies by abortion. Partial birth abortion reminds me, then in the spirit of Dredd Scott, of a slave-master taking the living baby of a slave mother and dashing his head against a rock or feeding her to an alligator. But is Senator Obama for partial birth abortion, he's for infanticide, for the death of "born alive" children outside the womb—children like Gianna Jensen who was "born during saline abortion". "Well into her third trimester of pregnancy, Gianna's biological mother was injected with a saline solution intended to induce a chemical abortion at a Los Angeles County abortion center. Eighteen hours later, and precious minutes before the abortionist's arrival, Gianna emerged. Premature and with severe injuries that resulted in cerebral palsy. But alive," (Ibid).But she lives today with cerebral palsy because her mother's saline abortion did not kill her. She told Daniel Allott, "I guess I don't die easy," In her own words to Sean Hannity and Alan Colmes, she lives because the abortionist was not there to "suffocate her." The nurse on duty sent her to the hospital. In that interview with Hannity and Colmes, she pointedly, passionately, and repeatedly reminded her hosts that Mr. Obama had repeatedly voted against legislation to keep her alive—an abortion survivor. Gianna was present when President Bush signed the Born

Alive Infants Protection Act in 2002. When Gianna was asked to reflect on Senator Obama's candidacy as President, she paused, then said, "I really hope the American people will have their eyes wide open and choose to be discerning… He is *extreme, extreme, extreme* (italics mine)," (Ibid). Senator Obama has consistenly denied that he voted against the Illinois version of the Infant Born Alive Protection Act. However, Mr. Obama "actually did vote against a version of the IL Born Alive Infants Protection Act that was identical to the federal version, contrary to multiple public statements Obama or his surrogates have made to rationalize his opposition to the IL bill for the past four years," Pro-Life Pulse, by Jill Stanek, http://www. jillstanek.com/archives/2008/08/breaking_ news_n_1.html, 8/13/08. New documents just obtained by National Right to Life Committee prove that Senator Obama has *for the past four years blatantly misrepresented his actions* (italics mine) on the IL Born-Alive Infants Protection bill. They "prove that in 2003, Barack Obama, as chairman of an IL state Senate committee, *voted down* (italics mine) a bill to protect live-born survivors of abortion—even after the panel had amended the bill to contain verbatim language, copied from a federal bill passed by

Congress without objection in 2002, explicitly foreclosing any impact on abortion. Obama's legislative actions in 2003—denying effective protection even to babies born alive during abortions—were contrary to the position taken on the same language by even the most liberal members of the Congress. The bill Obama killed was virtually identical to the federal bill that even **NARAL** (National Abortion Rights Action League) ultimately did not oppose," (Ibid). On Sunday, August 17, 2008 "Obama's campaign staff (finally) conceded to The New York Sun that Obama 'had voted against an identical bill in the state Senate.' The staff *tacitly* (italics mine) admitted that Obama has been misleading the public since 2004," <u>Media averts eyes as Obama caught in infanticide deception</u>, by Brian Fitzpatrick, OneNewsNow. com, 8/20/2008. Think about it this way: "But by arguing against the born-alive legislation because it might in some distant and ambiguous way obstruct abortion, Obama implies that *the right to an abortion triumphs an infant's right to life, even after he is born* (italics mine). Such logic is breathtaking, It says that even after birth, *a mother's right to rid herself of the baby supersedes any right that a child, now independent of the mother's body and domain,* *has a right to live,"* <u>Voters should be troubled by Obama's abortion stance</u>, by Dennis Byrne, Chicago Tribune, sec 1, pg 17, August 26, 2008.

Mr. Obama is for infanticide.

Mr. Obama's 10 Reasons for Supporting Infanticide

Following are 10 excuses Mr. Obama has given through the years for voting "present" and "no" on the IL Born Alive Infant Protection Act, or BAIPA

1. Introducing Born Alive was a ploy to overturn Roe v. Wade.

   a) There was no such amendment.

   b) Both definitions of "born alive" were identical—Illinois and Federal.

2. Sinking Born Alive was about outmaneuvering that political maneuver.

   a) Republicans loved to hold votes on "partial birth" and "born alive".

b) Republicans put the bills out to pigeonhole Democrats.

3. Introducing legislation to stop live aborted babies from being shelved to die with a political maneuver.

   a) The bill was unnecessary for Illinois.

   b) It was introduced for political reasons.

4. Aborting babies alive and letting them die violates no universal principle.

   a) More than Church teaching needed to ban born alive abortion.

   b) Must explain how abortion violates some principle that the faithful and people without faith are accessible to.

5. Aborting babies alive and letting them die is a religious issue.

   a) We live in a religiously pluralistic society.

b) I can't impose my religious views on another.

6. Mr. Obama apparently read medical charts and saw no proof.

   a) No documentation that hospitals were doing that charged.

   b)Accusations were baseless, no evidence.

7. Anyway, doctors don't do that.

   a) physicians are already required to care for abortion "born alives".

   b)physicians use life-saving measures for abortion "born alives".

8. Aborting babies alive and letting them die is a doctor's prerogative.

   a) Doctors are professional and objective

   b) Doctors know when a baby will live and when a baby will die.

9. A ban to stop aborted babies from being shelved to die would be burdensome to mothers.

   a) Mothers are already burdened.
   b) I will not allow any more burden to be put on women.

10. Babies who survive abortions are not protected by the Equal Protection Clause of the United States Constitution.

   a) The *only* speaker against BAIPA, March 30, 2001

   b) If the baby is a *person*, protected by Equal Protection Clause

(JillStanek,HTTP://WWW.WND.COM/INDEX.PHP?FA=PAGE. printable&pageID=45553)

Senator Obama is for infanticide. I call death by abortion "obamacide". He supports the misnamed Freedom of Choice Act, which will repeal all abortion restrictions previously gotten, including parental notification BEFORE a minor child can have an abortion. Mr. Obama will nominate pro abortion judges to the courts, especially the Supreme Court, to keep abortion legal—"rare" was stricken from this years Democratic platform. It has already been discussed that as President that in the interest of appeasement that Senator Obama might nominate Sen. Hillary Clinton to the bench. This would be a lifetime appointment for a still young woman who is philosophically a near clone of Senator Obama. In an eight year, two term presidency Mr. Obama could nominate at least three judges to the court. Philosophically, he would control the court for the next fifty years. Can America survive another holocaust----45,000,000 aborted babies over the next thirty-five years? Can Black America survive Planned Parenthood's genocide of another 15,000,000 aborted babies over the next thirty-five years? How would the Black community survive an eight year administration of America's first Black President?

IV. Mr. Obama and homosexuality & so-called "homosexual marriage"

We have ignored his position on homosexuality. Mr. Obama confesses that he is a Christian. For the Christian, the Bible is the final authority for the Believer. Although the Bible calls homosexuality "abomination", Senator Obama commits his full and unqualified support not only for domestic partnerships but for so-called "homosexual-marriage:" "obamination." He has promised to use the presidency as a "bully pulpit" to promote this policy including the repeal of former President Bill Clinton's "Don't Ask, Don't Tell" policy regarding gays in the military. To further reinforce so-called "homosexual marriage," Mr. Obama has committed to the repeal of the Clinton signed Defense of Marriage Act. All of this when AIDS is increasing uncontrollably both in the homosexual and Black communities, often with overlaps.

Senator Obama misunderstands and misrepresents Scripture to support his promotion of homosexuality by referencing the Sermon on the Mount. Listen to a written response of Pastor Clenard Childress, Jr. to Senator Obama:
Sen. Obama has written,

> "I am not willing to have the state deny American citizens a civil union that confers equivalent rights on such matters as hospital visitation or health insurance coverage simply because the people they love are of the same sex—nor am I willing to accept a reading of the Bible that considers an obscure line in Romans to be more defining of Christianity than the Sermon on the Mount."

(Before I begin Pastor Childress' response, please note that at no point does the Sermon on the Mount address the issue of homosexuality or same-sex issues. The only reference to sex is to the sacred sexual fidelity of a man and woman in marriage, and the caution to men that adultery originates in the human heart, Matthew 5:27-30).

Pastor Childress responds:

> "Sen. Obama, did you say obscure? That would tend to lead unlearned listeners to believe that the Bible is vague or obscure on the subject of homosexuality. Nothing could be further from the truth. Nearly half of the 32 verses in the first chapter of the New Testament book of Romans were dedicated to warning the early Church about sexual perversion. The Apostle Paul warned that perverse thinking and the habits they create were due to the fact that "they did not want to retain God in their knowledge."

That verse truly Reflects much of the cast in the Democratic Party.

I would like to ask Sen. Obama the question, "How obscure is this verse?" Leviticus 18:22 Thou shall not lie with mankind as with womankind: it is an <u>abomination.</u> That sounds pretty definitive to me. It would appear to me that Sen. Obama as well as many others shun and ignore the obvious and cloak the true causes of our problems." (Another obscure and indefinite passage is Leviticus 20:13 (RSV) "If a man lies with a male as with a woman both of them have committed an abomination; they shall be put to death, their blood is upon them." Likewise, one cannot ignore Genesis 18:16-19:29 where God destroys Sodom and Gomorrah for incendiary homosexuality).

Pastor Childress concludes his response to Sen. Obama: African Americans make up 12% of the population, but account for over 50% of all new cases of HIV. African American women account for a staggering 68% of all newly diagnosed HIV positive women in the United States. These women primarily contracted HIV from heterosexual sex. Now, with that said, 60% of all new aids cases in America will be the result of the violation of Leviticus 18:22 and Romans 1:27 (men having sex with men). Pastor Childress' concluding response to Sen. Obama does not include the overlooked impact of perinatal and pediatric aids, which affects Black babies and children.

The homosexual issue must not just address the public health issue of HIV/AIDS, it must also include the "Threat of MRSA infection increased by gay sex," http://www.onenewsnow.com/Journal/newsofinterest, 4/19/08. A recent study said sexually active homosexual men are far more likely to become infected with a new, dangerous, drug-resistant infection that is most often spread through skin-to-skin contact. Lead researcher Binh Diep of the University of California-San Francisco (after a study reports that) homosexual men are 13 times more likely to contract an MRSA infection. The disease is one of those that has been called a "flesh-eating bacteria" because the infection can become deeply imbedded in the soft tissue and muscle beneath the skin, causing permanent disfigurement and even death...Sexually active gay men, however, appear to be particularly susceptible to MRSA because anal sex can open fissures in the skin which allow the bacteria access to the body. According to an article in the New York Times, the new strain of MRSA is said to have "spread rapidly" in the gay communities in the cities examined by Diep, and "has the potential for rapid, nationwide dissemination" among homosexual men. Once this reaches the general population, it will be truly unstoppable," said Diep. "That's why we're trying to spread the message of prevention," (Ibid). The results were published in the February issue of the medical journal Annals of the Internal Medicine. www.reuters.com, 1/14/08; www.nytimes.com, 1/15/08; www.cnsnews.com, 1/12/08; and www. onenewsnow.com, 1/18/2008.

It must always be sincerely and truthfully stated that the motivation for publishing these concerns is not homophobia or some kind of irrational hatred against homosexuals.

It is noteworthy that even though Bishop Jakes and a group of pastors met with Mr. Obama he has been critical of Black churchmen and our position that differs from his. In an April 10 interview with *The Advocate* magazine Senator Barack Obama reportedly said "homophobic" messages are being proclaimed in the pulpits of Black churches because "most African-American churches are still fairly traditional in their interpretations of Scripture." However, he acknowledged that Dr. Jeremiah Wright, his former pastor was "very good on gay and lesbian issues," (CNSNews.com, 6/6/08).

Some Black pastors and leaders have responded

to Mr. Obama's remarks to *The Advocate*, rightly saying that Mr. Obama's positions contradict the fundamentals of the Christian faith. "The new definition of 'homophobic' means anyone who stands against homosexuality as a sin is homophobic," Pastor Ken Hutcherson of Antioch Bible Church in Redmond, Washington told *Cybercast News Service*. "That gives two choices to African-American pastors. They can either be Scriptural and demand righteousness from their flock, or they can drop Scripture and righteousness and support homosexuality," Obama Praised Wright, Criticized Traditional Black Churches on Homosexuality, by Penny Starr, CNSN News.com Senior Staff Writer, May 29, 2008. Mychal Massie, chairman of the Black conservative think tank Project 21, said following Christ's teaching doesn't make one homophobic. "The Christian church is called upon to subscribe to and be obedient to the will of God," Massie told *Cybercast News Service.* "That means there are absolutes. Embracing the homosexual while rejecting the act and immorality of homosexuality is not to be confused with or viewed as traditional or conservative. It is to be viewed as following the very 'Word of God'," (Ibid). "The Church is taught not to reject the personhood of practicing homosexuals due to the Scriptures teaching that they can be free from the detrimental lifestyle," Pastor Clenard H. Childress, Jr. of New Calvary Baptist Church in Montclair, N.J., and President of the Life Education and Resource Network, told *Cybercast News Service*, (Ibid). And a final perspective comes from Rev. Jesse Lee Peterson, President and founder of Brotherhood of a New Destiny (BOND), that Black "pastors should be talking to their parishioners about homosexuality. It makes them more aware of the truth about homosexuality and God's view on how we should deal with it," Peterson said. "It also causes them to realize what the Scriptures say about it." (Ibid). Rev. Peterson said Pastor Jeremiah Wright should not have been "celebrated for his preaching about homophobia in the black church." "Just because (Wright) speaks out in support of the homosexual lifestyle does not make him a leader in the eyes of most black Americans," Peterson said. "He may be a leader to angry liberal blacks and radical homosexuals, but not to the majority of churchgoing blacks," (Ibid.)

Senator Obama is not only for domestic partnership BUT for so-called "homosexual marriage" as well. Marriage since the 1970's is down 17% in America and in the Black community it's down by 34% and he's promised to use the presidency as a "bully pulpit" to promote both unrestricted abortion and protected homosexuality. Mr. Obama has promised to repeal former President Bill Clinton's "Don't Ask, Don't Tell" policy regarding homosexuals in the military. He's promised to repeal the Clinton signed Defense of Marriage Act. Can America and the Black community afford an increase in aids cases? Homosexual relationships can be legalized, but the consequences of that relationship cannot be stopped. Mr. Obama supports so-called hates crimes legislation, which will protect homosexuality from being challenged as an unacceptable, suicidal lifestyle. Hates-crime legislation is being used to intimidate opposition ideology, and ultimately it will be used to silence pulpits that preach against abortion and homosexuality.

V. Mr. Obama and Black issues

Ralph Nader has been a most perceptive critic of Mr. Obama. When Mr. Nader was asked the qualitative difference between Barack Obama, Al Gore or any other Democrat, he was very specific; "…he's deceiving people… There's only one thing different about Barack Obama when it comes to being a Democratic presidential candidate. He's half African-American. Whether that will make any difference, I don't know. I haven't heard him have a strong crackdown on economic exploitation in the ghettoes. Payday loans, predatory lending, asbestos, lead. What's keeping him from doing that? Is it because he wants to talk white? He doesn't want to appear like Jesse Jackson? We'll see all that play out in the next few months and if he gets elected afterwards," <u>Nader: Obama trying to 'talk white'</u>, by M. E. Sprengelmeyer, Rocky Mountain News, June 25, 2008.

When Mr. Nader was asked to explain "talk white, he quickly responded "Of course. I mean, first of all, the number one thing that a black American politician aspiring to the presidency should be is to candidly describe the plight of the poor, especially in the inner cities and the rural areas, and have a very detailed platform about how the poor is going to be defended by the law, is going to be protected by the law, and is going to be liberated by the law. Haven't heard a thing... I mean, the amount of economic exploitation in the ghettos is shocking. You'd think he'd propose a task force to at least study it. I mean, these people are eroded every day. The kids, bodies are asbestos and lead, municipal service discriminate against them because it's the poor area, including fire and police protection and building code enforcement. And then the lenders, the loan sharks get at them, and the dirty food ends up in the ghettos, like the contaminated meat. It's a dumping ground for shoddy merchandise. You don't see many credit unions there. This is, we're talking 40-50 million Americans who are predominantly African-Americans and Latinos. Anybody see that kind of campaigning? Have you seen him campaign in real poor areas of the city very frequently? No, he doesn't campaign there"

(Ibid). Not at a loss for words, Mr. Nader continues, "He wants to show that he is not a threatening, a political threatening, another politically threatening African-American politician…He wants to appeal to white guilt. You appeal to white guilt not by coming on as a black is beautiful, black is powerful. Basically, he's coming on as someone who is not going to threaten the white power structure, whether it's corporate or whether it's simply oligarchic. And they love it. Whites just eat it up," (Ibid).

Mr. Nader was right when he said that Mr. Obama cannot be considered a Black candidate because he does not speak on the issues that affect most Black people. In an election year where Black organizations are ratcheted up to do more registration of Blacks in states like Alabama and Georgia to help elect a Black President, it is done with the expectation that Blacks are more willing to vote for Blacks—sometimes their only votes. It is commonly discussed that Whites cannot be trusted to vote for Blacks, even for a Black like Tom Bradley of California, a David Dinkins of New York, or a Walter Braud of Illinois. Voting is a right, a privilege many people died for Black people to exercise. What has Senator Obama said or done about promoting/passing the permanent implementation of the 1964 Voting Rights Act rather than some kind of provisional limited extension? This is a shameful insult to Black people that we have to continue to lobby and beg for extension for that which we've paid for with sacrifice-- blood, tears, lynchings, and death. And it is a vulgar reminder of the hollow appreciation the United States has for the legacy of Dr. Martin Luther King, Jr. In a community of crippling illiteracy, high drop out rates, failing students in failing schools where is Senator Obama on strengthening and enforcing No Child Left Behind? Will he support vouchers to liberate Black children from the prison of failing schools that they might get the same quality education as Malia and Sasha? We know that he is Pro Choice for abortion. Will he be Pro Choice for schools? Blacks are heavy television watchers, what about consumer cable choice? Where is Mr. Obama on the environmental issue of chemical dumping, where the ghetto is used for businesses that work with chemicals, including landfills, dumps, and salvage yards?What about redlining and predatory lending, 400-600% interest payday loans, and increased home foreclosure? As columnist Charles Krauthammer said "For two decades you've had Republicans and Democrats in the Presidency and in Congress who have pushed to expand lending for housing for people who had not had it before --particularly African Americans who had been denied it because of discrimination and racism and (they) encouraged subprime loans which in the end collapsed," Fox News, 9/15/06. Therefore, Blacks have been adversely affected by the subprime situation. What about discriminatory loan practices that make it more difficult for Blacks to get into the housing market, and those who do at inequitable interest rates? Mr. Obama has talked some about HIV/AIDS, diabetes, and breast cancer BUT is he willing to look at reallocation of funds from research for AIDS—which is more preventable than treatable--to research for Diabetes, Blood pressure, Heart disease, breast/cervical/and prostrate cancer that's often congenital and ever increasing in the Black community? Mr. Obama's primary issues are primarily white woman issues. (Senator Obama was thrust into the forefront by Ms. Winfrey. If it is true that Ms. Ophra Winfrey, in the words of a Black woman "has made herself rich by catering to the pathologies of White women" but will not allow Sarah Pallin, a White woman, on her broadcast to "protect" Mr. Obama she's doing the same matriarch role that a Black woman would have done in slavery. White women in Florida have already started a boycott of her show.) The perception among some observers is that there is a campaign calculus that involves Obama making White audiences feel comfortable with him, while doling out straight talk to African-Americans," (***Essence,*** September 2008, page 156). This sentiment is echoed by Alvin Tillery, a Political Science professor at Rutgers University, in his comment that the old guard civil rights leaders can't complain publicly about Obama's approach "because they don't want to alienate a community that wants Obama to be president… But they are grumbling ," Tillery said. "There are a number of people who are disgruntled with his style of politics—a neo-Southern strategy. Keep black folks at a distance and keep white folks comfortable," <u>McCain making play at NAACP for votes Obama should win,</u> by William Douglas, McClatchy Newspapers, posted 7/13/08. A collateral, closing comment repeats this neo-Southern theme but adds that Senator Obama's "remarks are designed more to woo and soothe white voters than to *address issues impacting the African-American community* (Italics mine)", <u>Slam Dunk for Obama</u>, by Matt Friedman, OneNewsNow.com, 7/17/08).

White people, specifically Christians, do not have to use race not to vote for Mr. Obama. (According to current polling data, 40% of White Democrats are already planning to vote Republican). Rather, they, too, can use these same reasons to not vote for Mr. Obama as a Black Christian must consider. It's about positions not pigmentation. As a Black man, a Black father, a Black Christian, and as a Black Pastor I cannot and will not vote for Mr. Obama for President. I would like to be part of that historic moment, BUT . . .

VI. Conclusion

1. Mr. Obama is for unrestricted abortion. Abortion kills more Black people than all other forces in the Black community. Mr. Obama has promised that he will use the presidency as a "bully pulpit" to promote and defend abortion on demand. He has declared that his first official act would be to sign The Freedom of Choice Act, which would remove any and all limitations on abortion—partial birth abortions will be restored, parental notification requirements will be overruled, and post-abortion children who survive an abortion can be either be killed or left to die alone, in the dark in "comfort rooms." Let us not forget that across America 1452 Black babies are aborted daily, one Black baby "womb-lynched" every minute. Let us not forget that every Black baby aborted furthers the genocidal agenda of Margaret Sanger and

Planned Parenthood.Reproductive racism cannot be ignored whether preached by the Ku Klux Klan or implicitly supported by such notable civil rights groups as the National Association for the Advancement of Colored Peoples who accept abortion as an acceptable option and would not even allow the Macon, Georgia chapter to introduce a resolution on abortion. In the time it will take a voter to vote November 4th for pro-abortion Senator Barack Obama for President at least five Black babies will die.

2. For the record, Mr. Obama has already said "I don't want (my daughters*) punished with a baby* (italics mine)," The Audacity of Death," by Daniel Elliott, The Wall Street Journal Online, 6/5/08). If he would be consistent in his philosophy regarding a pregnant Malia and/or Sasha, he would take them to Planned Parenthood. As a father, he would abort his grandchild(ren). This father wants to be my President?

3. For Black people, abortion is more than just about "reproductive justice." Rather, it's more about "reproductive racism"

and genocide-- the planned, participatory death of not only the present generation but generations to come. According to the most recent census data Black Americans are no longer the largest U. S. minority population (U. S. Census Bureau.www. infoplease.com/ipa/A0762156.html.2007). How can we as a people continue to ignore the genocidal impact of abortion and accept the human devastation wreaked upon our community? Census is about counting. Dead Black babies don't count.

4. Related to abortion is not only the deadly impact upon the baby but the living impact upon the mother: "the potential for cervical cancer, breast cancer, fertility and psychological pain," <u>"Safe" Abortion</u>, page 9, Did You Know, Human Life Alliance © 2008. Abortion kills the baby and harms the mother. Both are human casualties.

5. Mr. Obama will appoint justices to the Supreme Court who will retain abortion on demand, and other like issues. He will appoint judges who will be " loose constructionists", even judicial activists, rather than "strict constructionists." In July,

2007 he spoke of his approach to picking judges: "We need someone who's got the heart…the empathy to understand what it's like to be poor or African-American or gay or disabled or old—and that's the criteria by which I'll be selecting my judges," by Daniel Henninger, WSJ.com, 6/6/08.They will have to pass a liberal "litmus test."Still a possible appointee is Senator Hillary Clinton, <u>Can you say 'Justice Hillary Clinton'?,</u> by Jody Brown, OneNewsNow. com, 6/19/08. These appointees will judge for the next fifty years. Abortion will never be ended.

6. Mr. Obama is not only for domestic partnerships, same sex relationships, but for so-called "homosexual marriage." Senator Obama has publicly committed to repeal the Defense of Marriage Act signed by President Clinton, which says marriage traditionally is only between a man and a woman. In like manner, Mr. Obama has promised to use the presidency as a "bully pulpit" to redefine marriage and promote so-called "same-sex marriages." Even though an inevitable consequence of these relationships is HIV/AIDS, this suicide

is encouraged and will be codified. (On September 17, Senator Obama flip flopped in a reported "interview with Mark Segal, publisher of the Philadelphia Gay News... Obama also declined to commit to have his attorney general support a lawsuit against the Defense of Marriage Act, which denies federal recognition of same-sex marriages and gives states the right to refuse to recognize such marriages. Obama said he's not sure the 1996 law would be overturned by the courts and he prefers a legislative solution," (Obama won't repeal "don't ask" on his own, by Nedra Pickler, OneNewsNow.com, 9/17/08). However, his heart's desire is still to overturn DOMA: "I support the complete repeal of the Defense of Marriage Act (DOMA)—a *position I have held since before arriving in the Senate* (italics mine)," Obama would use "bully pulpit" to advance homosexual agenda, Fred Jackson, OneNewsNow, 3/2008.

7. Mr. Obama is also for homosexual adoption. "We also have to do more to support and strengthen LGBT families," he wrote to Jennifer Chrisler, Executive Director of the Family Equality Council, after

the homosexual lobby group demanded his response after John McCain had answered no earlier.Mr. Obama continues, "Because equality in relationship, family, and adoption rights is not some abstract principle; it's about whether millions of LGBT Americans can finally live lives marked by dignity and freedom...That's why we have to repeal laws like the Defense of Marriage Act.That's why we have to eliminate discrimination against LGBT families. And that's why we have to extend equal treatment in our family and adoption laws," <u>Obama promises "change" for America one homosexual adoption at a time</u>, by Peter J. Smith, Lifesite News, 8/9/2008, OneNewsNow.com.

8. Senator Obama has declared his intention to repeal President Clinton's "Don't Ask, Don't Tell" policy implemented in 1993 regarding gays in the military. Mr. Obama's goal is to further normalize homosexuality. (On September 17, Senator Obama flip flopped in a reported "interview with Mark Segal, publisher of the Philadelphia Gay News... (that)if elected president he would not try to repeal the military's 'don't ask, don't tell'

policy on his own…My first obligation as the president is to make sure that I keep the American people safe and our military is functioning effectively," (<u>Obama won't repeal "don't ask" on his own</u>, by Nedra Pickler, OneNewsNow.com, 9/17/08). We must not forget, as President Mr. Obama will not relent until he has kept his promise to the gay community to undo the policy. And

9. Mr. Obama is for euthanasia, so-called mercy killing. Abortion is the killing of babies both in the womb and outside the womb. Euthanasia is killing the old, the sick who take resources rather than contribute to society. In 1857 the Dredd Scott decision declared that no slave had a right that a White man was bound to respect. In 1973 Roe v. Wade declared that no pre-born baby had a right that a mother was bound to respect. The euthanasists say that no sick or severely disabled person has a right to life that is bound to be respected—so that life is preserved. For the euthanasiasist quality of life determines whether life is worth preserving. Senator Obama is heard to have lamented that "voting for

legislation allowing Terri Schiavo's family to take it's case from state courts to federal courts in an effort to stop her euthanasia was his 'biggest mistake' in the Senate. Biggest mistake?" <u>The Audacity of Death</u>, by Daniel Allott, The Wall Street Journal Online, June 5, 2008. Mr. Obama does not believe that sanctity of life is as sacred as quality of life is desired. He has the spirit of Dr. Jack Kevorkian.

Blacks have been deceived before by ploys like "It's the economy, stupid!" There are some things more dear than the self-interest of personal economic well being. Slavery as an economic entity drove and divided the nation in another time. The economy and eugenics drive and divide America today. Our imperative must be the survival of a nation in a nation. For Blacks, then survival is not only about stopping the seemingly unending hemorrhage of abortion for America but the consequent genocide of Blacks. We must not be propelled to racial extinction by ever increasing abortion—sheep led to the slaughter by a Black sheep. For Black people who have survived slavery, endured segregation, and are now dealing with the lethal radon of systemic racism we've become so sensitive to the word discrimination that we've accepted abortion and justified homosexuality and defend it as a "civil right"—because the movement has convinced us that their sexual orientation is as unchangeable as our color and their condition is as congenital as our blood pressure and diabetes. To promote so called "homosexual-marriage" is suicide—killing Black men, Black women, and Black children. We cannot ignore the impact of HIV/AIDS on the Black family. Blacks cannot be distracted by the subjective issue of color.

Mr. Obama may be our "first" Black to be Democratic Party Presidential nominee, but does that mean that his first should be our first Black President?

Let me quote Pastor Ken Hutcherson of the Antioch Baptist Church again: "You can get excited about the first black man that's going to be the nominee (Mr. Obama was nominated by the Democrats for president and gave his acceptance speech August 28th). I mean, that's a first. You can get all excited about firsts.But, always think that the first should be someone that everyone is going to believe is capable of doing a great job. You don't want the first anybody or anything to end up being a bad choice and a bad influence and bad for America…When I look at what the first for the Democrats, (the) African-American that they have chosen, I'm excited about the first," Hutcherson concluded. "But I have no excitement about believing that that choice is going to best for America,"<u>Jakes continues to draw fire for Obama remarks,</u> by Jeff Johnson, OneNewsNow.com, 6/9/08).

It would be great and truly historic to see America elect her first Black President in my lifetime. However, not Mr. Obama, not now!! For the first Black President I would prefer a man or woman who values life from the womb to the tomb, and who understands marriage to be between only a man and a woman. As Bishop Jakes wrote, Senator Barack Hussein Obama's being selected as the Democratic Presidential nominee is a "historic accomplishment." However, we must not forget the words of Dr. Martin Luther King, Jr. that "Any success achieved at the expense of our children is no success," (Letter from a Birmingham Jail). Certainly, it is a great honor for Mr. Obama to be nominated. However, we must decide whether we will merely quote the words of Dr. King or whether we're willing to do what he and we ask White people to do. When you vote, will your decision be determined "by the content of character rather than the color of their skin"?

It is my belief that neither America nor the Black community can afford a Barack Obama presidency. Why not him? Why not now? Simply put:

Senator Barack Hussein Obama is

Black,
   But
      Not
         My
           Brother!

Donald William Johnson is a husband, father, President of TEAM Community Development Corp., and Pastor of Destiny Baptist Church of Rock Island, Illinois. Johnson is a graduate of Black Hawk College (A.A.), Moline, Illinois, American Baptist College of the Bible (B.A), Nashville, Tennessee and Southern Baptist Theological Seminary (M. Div.), Louisville, Kentucky. He also attended Augustana College, Rock Island, Illinois and Howard University School of Religion, Washington, D. C.

Donald William Johnson worked for the American Bible Society and the Home Mission Board of the Southern Baptist Convention in Atlanta before pastoring New Faith Baptist Church, Park Forest, Illinois, Mt. Olive Baptist Church, Joliet, Illinois, and now Destiny Baptist Church, Rock Island, Illinois. He was a board member for the Home Mission Board of the Progressive National Baptist Convention; Vice Chairman of QC Chapter of Congress of Racial Equality; Vice President of the Iowa Illinois Bi-State Chapter of the Southern Christian Leadership Conference; and board member of the Metro-Com Branch, National Association for the Advancement of Colored Peoples. Johnson served as Assistant to the President at Chicago

Baptist Institute, Chicago, Illinois where he also taught for over ten years. Although a Pastor, this book is written as a private citizen, who is a Black Christian.